D.E. STEVENSON

Ancestors
and Other Visitors

Selected Poetry & Drawings

UNAM
PRESS
UNIVERSITY OF NAMIBIA

University of Namibia Press
www.unam.edu.na/unam-press
unampress@unam.na
Private Bag 13301
Windhoek
Namibia

first published in 2018

poetry, drawings, design and layout: don stevenson
painting, "Ancestral Presence": tuli mekondjo, with kind permission

typography consultant: niina turtola

inspiration: edward e., robert, william b., rosemarie, jennifer, roya, daniel, unotjarii, joree, christopher, donald john, uncle bill, first rain dance, muhapikwa

set in American Garamond, 12 and 14 point

ISBN 978-99916-42-44-4 (print paperback)

ISBN 978-99916-42-45-1 (e version)

Distribution
In Namibia by Namibia Book Market: www.namibiabooks.com
Internationally by the African Books Collective: www.africanbookscollective.com

Contents

TO MY BROTHER
Danny Clifford Stevenson
July 1958–June 1962

FOREWORD

Thoughtful, challenging and often complex, this unusual collection of poems, written in the space of 65 months, distills 71 years of life experience in 74 poems.

Most of the poems appear to transcend form: mostly in free verse, many employ internal rhyme. Sometimes long, often written in stanzas, they are best read aloud for their musicality to be appreciated.

Unlike a lot of Namibian poetry, the volume is not grounded in the Namibian historical experience or in post-independence themes of disillusionment and social critique, with a few exceptions like 'Walker'. This thematic difference is understandable given the poet's background; it is even refreshingly original.

Stevenson seems to take as his credo, or mantra, the quotation that heads section 2.

The contemporary pilgrim is a person separated from the life-infusing myths that supported tribal man... Today, each man must work at telling his own story if he is to be able to reclaim his personal identity. (Kopp, S.)

Stevenson is that pilgrim, telling his own story, highlighting people and relationships over time in the diverse settings of America, Europe and Namibia, trying at the same time to understand Namibian realities and developing his own response.

Stevenson acknowledges e. e. cummings and W. B. Yeats as poetic mentors, and the careful reader can trace these influences. A few poems are influenced by cummings' style, such as 'a day's wet child'.

The Irish poet W. B. Yeats' influence can be seen in Stevenson's empathy with themes in Yeats' poetry (particularly aging) and with his mysticism. Mystical would seem to describe Stevenson's natural orientation in life and several poems reflect this orientation, particularly 'God be the Glory' and 'Promised'. The most obvious reference to Yeats is found in 'A Personal Bethlehem', a written reply to Yeats' 'The Second Coming'.

Robert Hayden is a spiritual mentor to Stevenson. Hayden, a Bahá'í by confession, used different approaches when referencing religious faith in his poetry, sometimes direct, at other times oblique. Stevenson follows this example.

"Genuine poetry can communicate before it is understood." So said the 20th century poet, T.S. Eliot. In order to grasp or interpret many of the poems in this collection, readers may need time and thought to access them. Often they communicate through mood and inference rather than explicit reference. The imagery is sophisticated and powerful, and sometimes shocking.

They are, at one and the same time, philosophical and enigmatic, simple and complex, serious and ironic—they invite reading and re-reading. For several poems the poet has included notes which offer context or references.

My personal favourite, 'love is', closes with the lines:

draw deeply breath
once love lost will return
some eternity to hold
or to haunt you

—Helen Vale, former senior lecturer, literature
University of Namibia

Section 1

Of Love & Life

I hope that you, whom I have loved,
will find me in your memories and smile
even as I
 when I remember you

—D. Stevenson
'Memories'

Heart's path

The road carries him
through blazing heat
through nagging wind
through grassy fields
where warthogs run.
Takes him on Sunday
places he's never been
nor ever dreamt
to quiet people of dark skin
of joyful hearts
of grieving hearts.
A long road of bitumen
one of gravel
one of sand
one whispered Name
and felt the pull
of heart's path.

Mother speaks

I   drift
we wander
reaching out, but rarely touching
I'm looking for something
searching for a partner
        and someone to own my children

Is there a remover for this difficulty?
I need to say
            Blessed is the heart
            that's tight as a fist!
            Blessed are the arms
            that hold a child!
Open wide yours and embrace me
and I will embrace you

Help me stop, stop weeping
Help me find a way, so we
        won't drift
        won't wander
will find the same thing
and be someone
        to own our children.

a day's wet child

Arriving
not unlike a child
birthed, gently had
surely smiled
from parents, her artful hiding
found the child wet
    after suddenly
        the sky opened

Insinuating
like a vine among her thighs
he sat long for waiting
while the child grew older
becoming wise and wetter still
as small hands to earth do fall
    (she flowered
        lush and parting)

Anticipating
women of women born
generations gifted
fully formed
as from fecund loins
were spawned
    (the rain) for yet another
        wettest child

Warrior steps out of shadow into the light
pencil

misplaced

i recognised the wide invitation
   to touch you
the need of warmth and protection
consumed by the stronger
and naked affection wept
but was not wet enough
      to douse that fire

in a tarnished mirror
   our likewise deserted selves
fisted hard in loins
drive us through the angry world
and mean to crash our busted hearts
      careening down the potholed slope
        of our desire

somehow we got misplaced
when, on a loveless road
a mother or a father
abandoned the wide-eyed child
     who needed only to be held

southbound

Southbound on rails
you sway upon a window seat
the towel draped over your head
          conceals dark eyes
so I watch your nose
     move as you speak—
"I'll look different without my hair,"
you say.

Yes, I say, you will
        look like you do
only without hair.

A smile walks across your face
     as you catch my drift and
looking down at your tethered feet,
    I say,
so, where do you think you're going?

"Oh, I don't know," you say, "wherever,
it's worth going, I suppose." [1]

[1] Looking out the window at the world
you don't seem to comprehend, I know
you don't mean that, because tomorrow
you'll do the same thing you did yesterday
and unleash your 'lectric curls
to keep the boys at bay.

Havana mosaic

Sunlight and shadow dance
on a discarded washing machine
useless here, yet like the Rock
of Gibraltar rising
below, a red blue yellow green blanket
airing and dusty
arranged nicely with broken furniture,
a rusted petrol drum in company.

Coils of wire grace popping roofs
sheet-metal corrugate under midday sun,
a tragic car—no glass, no wheels

the houses grew around it
won't be pushed out or past
a rusty frame (once a bed)
against the neighbor's
bedroom shed.

An imperceptible breeze
(unnecessary in the joyless air)
dries her hand-wrung wash
on crisscrossed lines under poison trees
beside her metal house—as such
unbearable
            after sunrise
                after October

any time, in fact
but on an early summer's eve.

named for a dream
(to Roya)

A child at the fulcrum,
sentinel to justice and fair play,
she had a thankless job to fill:
some cosmic balance pushed her
from the midst of Libra days.

I remember the young girl, pacing
back to forth over sunlit fields
commanding a host of visioned friends
whom she rallied with an artist's will
brandishing a sun's invisible shields.

She and I got into wool at times
like souls find sport in altercation
occupying a small space at the time
we grew beyond scraps, affirming
spirit binds true in any occupation.

A young woman in the crucible
clock hands spinning, the line twixt laundry
and essentials blurs while children grow
she gathers the next version of home
headstrong, never yielding to quand'ry.

How she balances the day-to-day
with the artist, earns admiration
she pilots menus and rehearsals,
negotiates chicanes and hair pins,
the road *she* paved with expectation.

Friends' admiring eyes shine brighter still
when fire-juggling feats are mentioned;
cheering flags slap hard against the wind
witness to the lion heart that beats
in her Gibraltar of intention.

When the bagger man

When the bagger man comes for me
I take off my thoughts and place them
carefully, in the drawer with my socks.
I'll be needing them later to cover my tracks
and socks will serve well, those track-covering thoughts.

When my companion for life assesses me, knowing
not what I'm about, I understand her implied question:
"Where do you think you're going?", and would like to say...
but am afraid to come up, precisely on that day,
late and a holler short.

When my Herero friend calls out at night
I know why: she wants the meat on the bones
someone neglected to eat
at the feast—when family, whispering, arranged a wedding
to the cousin who came, just to shake her acquaintance.

When my clumsy cute muse holds out on me
I get to fussing, 'cause I don't understand her moods
and just now, she ain't talking.
That piece? it should've fallen from the sky by now
but she just laughs as I, to her, go crawling.

When my musician friend stands in the drive, politely smoking
I realise for the first time, something melodically important:
no matter how hurt or sad the passing world, I will die
        knowing, I am an artist and a poet
and everyone who counts will know it, too.

A love missed
does not exist
only the pain
of its absence

Love lacking existence
should end pain
and absence or presence
no longer exist

The mind losing its grasp
slips and
the question of these things
no longer persists

Yet in their persistence
proof
that time alone exists
in non-existence

Why life does not stop
begs explanation
for I do not exist
only the pain

of her absence

i do not exist

World war
for Donald John

We were, in our world
    a war
too caught up in your marriage
for a child to see clearly
the life that brought you to me
    or me to you
depending on one's point of view

Had I been older
I might have cried for you
    (living your death)
but did only for myself, angrily
beneath the weight
    of your proximity

Did we meet
on fields of destruction
was there no rain
no washing of blood in our veins?
You've been gone some time now
    and we don't talk, obviously

But still I remember
cease-fires in our war of attrition
    and a place
where you and I might yet embrace
    as friends

Venus

Not quite black or brown or white
lace brows
    not quite fixed
to her chiseled face
    will not stop
they drift, a vision
       over their appointed place
Never
have apparitions of dark flame
      lifted a precipice above
smoldering soul frames
to a raging crown

An intruder's heart
      only just smitten
bids relief
from persistent fire
or should burn
      and burn away
before death's dull mission
    to
      escape

here there

wrote his love,
are you there?
whereupon
he responded, i am there now,
        meaning here,
        where i am right there
        wherever either is;
        though was neither here
        nor there
        when you enquired
        if i were there
        which is
        where i am
        wherever
        where is
        if ever
        you should again, whereto
                his love responded
                yes, i understand
                i was lost
                thinking
                i'd found you,
                yet found only
                that i wasn't
                quite there where
                you write from
                but were not
                when I enquired
                of your
                thereabouts

Thrice in a lifetime
after 'Once In a Lifetime', Talking Heads
ball pen on ghosted digital collage

love is a thing
forever, even
after it's passed

betray it, spurn it
whose voice still echoes
eons after it's crashed

and that which was
though failing to stick
still is

to the inscrutable Mind
whatever lives or ever has
will always be

draw deeply breath
once love lost will return
some eternity to hold

or to haunt you

Christmas day #2

Christmas day
the year of their Lord
two thousand sixteen
the pluviophiles rose
from dusty graves
to frolic as the streets ran
and gutters could not hold
and cats took refuge
on the mats of chosen doors

Standing silent
all thought shut
I watch cascades of wind
blown water
soaking the world, garden
and working clothes
remove an obstruction from
drum-down overflows
the land awake

Ancestral Presence
Tuli Mekondjo, acrylic paint, paint markers and permnanent markers

Section 2

Ancestors
& Other Visitors

The contemporary pilgrim is a person separated from the life-infusing myths that supported tribal man. He is a secular isolate celebrating the wake of a dead God. When God lived, and man belonged, psychology was no more than "a minor branch of the art of story-telling and mythmaking." Today, each man must work at telling his own story if he is to be able to reclaim his personal identity.

Kopp, Sheldon B. (1972). *If you meet the Buddha on the Road, Kill Him: The Pilgrimage of Psychotherapy Patients*

Muhapikwa
an imagined conversation

Burning fiercely, she stood before a full house in the FNCC gallery—poised, she spoke her mind and I felt the point in her argument.

"I can see you," I blurted.

She retorted, "Do you really? Don't you think I'm stupid? People *say* I'm stupid."

"Which people? So, they met you, they heard your voice?"

"No, but *you* heard it, since I chose to be here and you took up the invitation to come see the film."

"Honestly, I see you. I'm surprised to find you in this dark and unfriendly space! Your voice resonates between the walls, ceiling and floor: all concrete!
     Isn't that amazing?"

"Walls don't make a prison. Darkness? It can't dim my sight; concrete can't chill my heart."

"I can't even *imagine* you, I mean, here, in this place. It doesn't make sense!"

"Strange! Is that why you take so many pictures of us? *Tara kombanda*! Look up! What did you expect to see?"

"No offense, but you're dirty. They say you don't bathe."

"What, 'they'? What do *they* know about my circumstances?"

"And look at how you dress! Very interesting but, it's said you're backward and superstitious."

"Tell me, who are these judges?"

"People misjudge you, because they can't understand your language; they don't get your sense of humor, don't recognise the bite of your wit!"

"So why did *you* come here, to hear someone speak the
strange language, to see a woman with bare breasts?"

"I just came to see a movie; I didn't expect to find *you* here!
But OK, I stuck around because, well, I was curious...
I was drawn to your table, but feel uncomfortable looking
you in the eye. I keep checking the trinkets you've spread
out, because you could cast a spell, you know,
bewitch me...
    Ok, maybe they're not, trinkets..."

"*Tara kombanda*!
I've crossed worlds to be here.
I risk my dignity just standing in front of you!
I have no anger, nor do I resist change, only lopsided notions
of progress."

"You say that, but is it possible?"

"If not for the king and sovereign of this world,
    we would all disappear!
Okutja paturura omehoue!"
    Just open your eyes!

Strangely familiar now, the fire in *her* eyes and the voice
that leaps from the walls, the wicked smile
that lights up the room.

"*Taare ko u ua uandje*
Tare ozondjise zandje ndozo nde nda ndenoo muriro ko maendero
za uoo Ndji tare naua Ourainga uandje, oudjenje uandje nozo
mbanda zandje ndaungurua no mukova uo gombe, omasa nguyeri
morutu ruandje.
Ouami ngubiri Muhapikua."

"Look at me, behold my ochre beauty!
Behold my long braids that flare at the ends.
Behold...
    my shells, my rings, my leather,
my naked power!

"I am
    Muhapikwa."

no telling apart

For centuries the Ovaherero have
spoken to their ancestors, a practice
that has fallen into disfavor with
many of them.

Enchanted, a worm scar
has earned its royal due
bearing battle-torn missives from night

to jump a shade she sees, for truth,
what cannot be and conceals others
she would likewise keep from sight.

She shares the world with shadows
in the company of a child
who became her greatest grandmother.

Disfigurement guides her hand at art
and from the occasional dead (who whisper)
she shall never stand apart

nor claim distance in her days
nor tell their world's insistence
from her closest family ways.

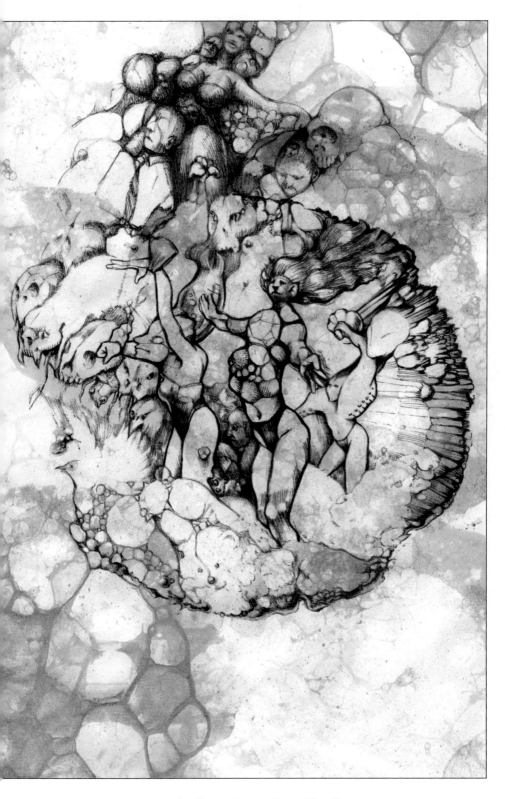

Fourth-dimension visitors *(detail)*
ball pen on soap-solution painting from a kindergarten class

sing for us

Awaited like the rain
you stood to become the next born:
gifted, a child the ancestors
had surely smiled upon.

Women of your line are strong
perhaps, waiting only to be called upon
for you remembered and summoned her,
Joree Tjiharuka, your great grandmother.

A child woman, she would not die!
Though eight years old and alone
in the wilderness she survived
so you could be born.

Not to be forgotten,
she who took flight is yet illumined—
in soiled dresses
scornful of daylight.

Her red clay locks laugh as she runs
She eats berries to stay alive
No water! but what can be sucked
from fruit she finds hidden in the earth.

Though with deaf ears
we listen
Joree may still sing for us
and by her song we may yet remember

When proud women flew on feathered feet
over rock and grasses
no songs, no dances
but those of love and grace to carry them.

Warriors in the dark

Combat with formless dark
    is done
by warriors dancing with the sun:
creating air and water
    from the fire
as they sweep fierce arc
      through turbulent sky, no longer dark.

In their wake
the fruit of labour is brilliant blue
    confirming the light
giving birth to rainbows
    and the gold wonder of bees
whose ecstatic dance doth promise
    the heady froth of mead.

Purple mountains, fires within
    leap to ash, exploding
    white hot, in violent din
send warriors across a black
    and barren plain
as earth, in cooling, doth buckle
    her coastal shelves to raise.

Eyes ablaze in crimson
    they do gaze with eagles' sight
as melody is loosed in heaven
    on tips of wings in flight.
High above—now amber plain,
where our ancestors will school the young
    in ways of migrating bison—

the song of world has just begun.

I am African woman

I am African woman,
from this day forward,
a victim of no one.
My would-be tormentor,
    an inglorious past,
shall make no claim
for I refuse to do
what it commands me to.

Ach! this African woman!

I am Eve, first woman,
first wife.
Despite the past's intrusion
or a husband's fornication
infidelity shall exercise no dominion
but to pronounce man's
    expulsion
from the garden of Eden.
So say I, an African woman.

Revealed (ancestral reflection #4)

*The bible says we shouldn't communicate
with the dead, yet speaking to our ancestors,
especially when we are nearing death, is
common for my people... sms, 7 June 2013*

In the Book stands revealed
thou shalt eschew counsel
with familiar spirits
walk not in darkness
deny charmers and wizards
cast out dread.

Down millennia
your ancestors braved
similar corridors
We should believe that they,
    in superstitious ways,
were lost to darkness,
by shamans mislead.

Who, then, shall reveal for them
truths that lie
beyond their ancient borders?
Not you, not I.

Yet you and I stand poised
at once removed from alien states
deplored, without grace
to respond to questions posed
    in latter days:
Do we walk in paths of righteousness
or do we pick and choose from the Book
only counsel we find mellifluous?
What, indeed, is the measure of our faith?

Arc magnificent

brothers, sisters quicken
    in a cool gloom resounding
gliding on feet magnificent,
intrepid hearts are pounding
to the earth rising in loins and limb
they summon vexing ancestors
    or quash the beast within

with widening arcs,
they circle in delirious flight,
resurrect ages from a dimming past
sprinkle incantations with delight
    or foretell our possible futures

wretched clans receive
no truth from history
nor espouse:
    a gravely was
    a pounding is
    a rhythm in the body
it's a stillborn tragedy

in another court
    (power and poetry)
feathered dancers conjoin
an other-worldly host
in union with all things
synchronous
was and when and why

sisters, brothers
your spell thunderous dance
with leaping does recall us
from lives stuck, for love askance

of disremembered spooning
of mystery
    or
        never risked
of ancient spells flung off
and lost to current circumstance.

Tell me, how should we remember
who we were
    or are
        or might be?
Should we hearken to our feral kin
in fearsome night complaining?

Sand

A sovereign south easterly
hammers nettled exteriors,
stuccoed rooms witnessed little
after spirits left but the vacated,
the intermittent (roofs) and the sand (inundated)
her swinging windows and seized doors
testify a century vanity in flaking paint
and stones ago.

Stranded on silenced ways our lady,
the desert claims
hour by hour, her dead
not embraced or raised
shriek abandoned back
at stinging winds
insidious through naked frames
howling her to ruin.

in blood and earth

A memory of earth
is handed down, mother to daughter
    in the ceremony of survival

For the child forced to run or die,
no hand was lifted in protection,
yet she did, run to live
and daughters do remember.

Sometimes a heart deafens
and a voice breaking deep and dark,
calls to them, "Do you hear my blood
coursing in your veins?
Do not, do not forget,
    we are Herero!"

As I sit up nights

As I sit up nights with waking
a Hand caresses fevered thought
and with a gentle touch all fire
of heaven, fiends and angels bought
yet borrowed against the glowing iron
only warmth, despite all these
though deep and true and devastating
they presume to be

Worlds ancient and afar, are clasped
as on that bright field
all time and distance, to one moment
    are distilled,
yet for that immeasurable time,
        shall never pass

Walker

A walker down our street
called me mister
and asked respectfully
were there no shoes I'd forgotten
      now perhaps remembered
to replace these disintegrating
or trousers
to pull over the holes he was wearing?
Though he was small of stature.

I did not feel grand
passing them on
(my drawers are full of tumble)
but I felt better sitting on the curb
as he tried them on:
shoes and trou too large,
      "no, it doesn't matter
paper in the toes will fit them fine,"
(to sit comfortable).

He walked on then,
a sack of video cassettes over his arm,
I, not at all a better man
he, a man slightly better off.

Poison the seed

You could poison the seed, shatter the hearth
out of spite or love and I would not chastise (you)
my tufted titmouse

You could slander family name or tear to shreds
enduring legacies and I would not disown (you)
my sacred dandelion

You could wreck a century of building or squander
a king's ransom and I would not curse (you)
my dove, o love for life

You could burn fields at harvest, spoil silos in store
with a plague's rot and I would salvage your share
my sleek sable

You might wallow in gutters, ply a tramp's trade
and I would embrace (you)
O rose of my heart

You could cry insurrection ten lord and law
ruin palaces or parliament and I would defend (you)
my sweetest child

You could curse God and angels, deny the kingdom
and my home would still be (discretely) yourn
my dearest daughter

New World

She asks for rain
        It arrives in buckets
She marvels at fulfillment
      of everything she ever wanted
               no doubt   beyond tomorrow
she'll walk the cliffs above a green ocean
shedding preconceived ideas
about devotion   no doubt   will deliver her
to another precipice above a different ocean
on the shores of other continents.

    She sees
straight through the mist that locks the coast
    and opens
her thighs to a ghost who takes her body as a token
that will conceive a new age and new people
    She asks
    She sees
    She opens
        Don't think hers, a tenuous grasp of morality
It was ordained
    It is her destiny
           to give birth to the world

Ndapandula

In the dark
He won't take eyes off you.
Though ashen skin hides
The assertion of melanin
Your impending passage
Summons would-be husbands
Uncertain, you should take one.

Swelling breasts foretell
An end to maidenhood
     —she guides you—
To this crossroad on a woman's journey.
The lashed hawk may peck your eyes out
Should you mock its insistence
Or call on Christ Jesus.

Look up, dark girl, don't pretend
Smeared naked you are invisible
Glorious ghost, you cannot
Escape longing
It stirs life in dead wood
And pulls him down, unknowing
Among the corn.

Should you start to unravel,
Touch yourself, gently;
The ancestors whisper, Ndapandula,
Shades who may nod to
Missionaries still bless efundula
    whispering,
Lie down, the corn is greening.

Ndapandula *(detail of work in progress)*
Tuli Mekondjo and D. Stevenson
permanent markers and acrylic on canvas

Unseen

I am witness nr. 31
to a re-enactment
of Namibia's holocaust
(30 years before the sequel)
by great granddaughters
and grandsons
in a fortress
that denied existence
to bantu settlers in their adopted
homeland
dust gone to wind
unseen
by a metal horseman

Omaere

Whenever
that affection
rises
with a bright day's
dawning
it sours like milk
on an afternoon
slowly
to Omaere
my tongue is burning

Section 3

Faith

Bahá'u'lláh:
Logos, poet, cosmic hero, surgeon, architect
of our hope of peace,...

I bear Him witness now:
towards Him our history in its disastrous quest
for meaning is impelled.

—Robert Hayden
'Words in the Mourning Time'

inevitably confused

Cherishing
the human condition
as I certainly do
I willfully embrace confusion
taking a spin in the tumbler
in an ill-advised rejection
of arrangements sane and sensible
—the fool rushes in—regrettably
no angel will accompany
for fear of treading
with objectionable feet
on the feet of those in company
who sit upon the seat
of confounded rationality.

moments of Siyyid-i-Báb

He came in the eternal moment of His death
with assurance, I had been rewarded
regardless of my unbecoming.
It seems the Almighty favours cutting slack
when we leap with audacity.

He came at a time of headlessness, I
savoring illusion, dwelt with the unacceptable
dropping like a stone to be born again
yet for all my guarded secrecy
still languished, a guarded fool.

He came minutes after sunrise
with razor light and firm reminder:
in life as in death, in fall or in flight
you pay for what you get, and it's woolly
out there in traffic.

As the world marries

Reaching for a Hand
to hold ours, trembling
we take uncertain steps
on a journey of remembering
seeking vision
    perhaps protection,
unaccustomed to light
we stumble from the night
into glimpses of perfection

        knowing somewhere
        within that
        the supernal One
            illumines the path
        and bestows instruction
        guiding us out the mess
        we are continuously producing,
        diverting inevitability
        of destruction

        Averted by a Greater Will,
Whose purpose, unwavering, fulfills
not in step with our want of understanding
but in the loom of a System
passionately weaving order
in whose soft folds, cradled,
    we fall to love
and marry across our world's
    now falling borders

Magus (Who awakens)

Ancient Magus
Primal Poet
stir now truant hearts,
who may become your lovers
once roused, will seek out others
who shall likewise quit their sleep
to discover
the One bequeathed.

You call upon our rooms
to find us in unbecoming attire
on couches of forgetting
wrapped in our desire
awaiting an apt Physician
a Light-conjurer, a Magician
Who will heal the wound
in a spasm of delight.

You lean in close, to whisper:

Grant, dear sleeper,
a slight air at your ear
for you can nary picture

       Me

in your dream.
Awaken then
catch accents of My honeyed Tongue.
You'll desire nothing else
as for the first time you see collapsing
your dear, but petty necessity
above which you may rise
to find supreme felicity.

Áqá Khán

A thousand
nay, fifty thousand, and more
press close.
Repelled not by fetid breath,
your dark decay of soul,
for they are compelled to lay anguish
at the feet of your foul intent.
Birthed in misplaced blame
your despicable act meant to kill
or break by weight of chain
      Him
Who is the Desire of the World.

That world would crush you,
but is held at bay by Him
Who bears witness to all deeds.
The soul's dissipation in oblivion
would be a loving mercy
but you shall not enjoy that calm
      or release
from your chosen place in history,
captive to the unthinkable,
      Mírzá Áqá Khán.

Suspended in a timeless state,
embracing a link of chain,
Qará-Guhar, by name,
you shall recall each moment
what He bore by your decree,
miscalculated for neither did He
break nor expire.
But as sure as fuel feeds fire, was lifted
as Christ upon the cross, forgiving

47

what they could not comprehend
indeed, as you did not.

Hold dearly the iron
　　　to your chest, Áqá Khán,
for truth it is unique, a weighty blessing
and the one thing
that connects you to Him:
　　　through wretched misery
　　　to luminous victory.

celebration

There he is, the old man
who frequents all the usual venues
whose voice drifts down the hall
calling for laundry,
only to disappear
behind a higher purpose.

Listen to our daily celebration
of awesome mediocrity:
a call to champion splendid boredom
with accolades to the perpetually bland.
Indeed, the old man frequents every-
and anywhere he is called to be.

We shall raise a glass
to the death of excellence
with homage to the commonplace,
and yet, fail to recognise
miraculous, it goes unnoticed
right before our eyes.

Quietude

quietude drops
over a cloudless
thursday morning

rattle in his breathing, a fine day
knowing not whether grace will carry
him gently yet firmly
      away

though children dance
of carefree notions, he
a child, too, 'neath immaculate sky

turns breath on a point
his sole devotion,
almost eternity at the door

of time and space
not much are left
as it swings shut
      to open

leaves

silent yellow leaves
gather at the door this morn
a sparrow has flown

Genesis 1:7 *(detail)*
ball pen with digital enhancement

God be the Glory

God be the Glory
on a north-bound bakkie
God be silence
over scorched earth south of Keetmans
God be open sky
a promised host descending
God be womb and ant and seed
and blossoms to the fruiting
God be light in newborn eyes
to a world of stories
and our coming of age
God be the Glory

passing through

i am not hungry in the usual sense
i move about, bone beneath sufficient flesh
a vexing obsession with honesty
gnaws at the physical, somewhere between
my gut and gravity

maybe my life's a prayer, it could be a poem
or better claimed: a persistent dream
i've been spending, as if it would never end
catching a glint of moonlight through a tear
in the world (it wouldn't bend)

i am not averse to confessing
i'm a bit scared, aren't *you*?
though i have on good authority, life
is not terminal at the stone,
have you ever spoken to anyone
on a second time through?

Mount Sea

A wrathful mountain
rises above a riverless plain
beyond no foothills of regret
ferocious water bids me scale
and scale I would attempt,

placing each foot after the other
wading is slow
despite a holy compulsion deep
(that raised this height, and buoys me)

I haven't faith to climb the sea

If I should

Early sun fall on ceramic tiles
leaf shadow wide across cherry wood
and where wood meets tile
a strip of peeled veneer
reveals the woodworm gone

My heart lifts in the moment
a song, if I should
just pause
         for one

Supplied (precise in His attendance)
with every good thing sent down
assured a century back
what comfort in this
what silence!

A Personal Bethlehem

The world ended today (or maybe yesterday).
There was no point, for her to carry on;
Things fall apart: vexed by demon time—
Banks defraud, countries are closing.
Yet, it is only blindness or anger that compels our denial
For the end did not come as it was supposed to.

Shall we ponder this, shall we commit to action
Or merely watch the cripple, as she lumbers on
Without our intervention?
If only a vagrant clown in company
Should we trundle through the mayhem, greed and anarchy
Loosed upon the world.

Fall from self-righteous skies, riders of apocalypse
Wolves in clothing, you console your sheep
Even as you lead them into the maw of random prophecy.
Sounding anthems to that conceit,
The multitude, unwitting, rushes forth to complete
A greater scheme, and destroy the house once holy.

Fall from shari'ah skies, riders of apocalypse.
Beasts in masks, you abduct daughters
And slay brothers in the name of the Father.
Hostage to a poisoned history, you enslave and inter
In the scorched and ancient earth
To seed a nation without mercy or compassion.

Fall from petroleum skies, riders of apocalypse,
Faceless in Armani, you hide in corporate labyrinths
Clutching blood-sodden reigns,
You hold us hostage, demanding to be paid,
As you slouch towards Bethlehem,
Long since the Second Coming was mislaid.

My house door

My house door tends to shut
            on the wind
and on each imperceptible breeze
            launches a mission
slinging its arc when the stop
            has marched mysteriously
                        out of position.

Steering clear it begins its rotation
            on a finely-attended hinge
building angular velocity as it sweeps
            to a predetermined destination
with a distinctive crash
            of wood rattling wood
                        it proclaims determination.

Oh, could I swing so easily
            facing the loss of viability
How little it worries me
            to foresee no predictable income
thinking: It is impeccable history
            that prompts belief
                        perhaps naively:

when a door shuts, another opens.

Prisoners

The sun comes up,
    again
strangely, I shrink from prayer
contemplating a legion of prisoners
shackled, tortured
    and denied
        justice
whose death is publicly deplored
yet privately forgotten
even as miracles I've observed
not the smallest of which is : FACT
I have yet to be exposed
for shrinking from the consequence
of faith   and loss   and love.

How many the faithful (who may NOT BREAK),
must bend beneath the weight of chain and scourge of stocks
until we see? We need only wake up from our dreams
of convenience, comfort and the daily bread.

How many the dogs that snarl
or dig up the earth of vain friendship
to comprehend : there is no cake at the celebration
    of martyrs?
Only the sun coming up,
    again
and a walk through blazing corridors
    and REDEMPTION
which they purchase from their damp and glorious
prison.

Rumi

I am lost in Rumi
I thought he would
deliver me from confusion
then he left
me standing in the road
not knowing if I should
forge north or south.
I felt betrayed
then remembered
the mystic's duty:
He is not on the road
to be followed.

Rumi could be lost, too.

Heart's Desire

The heart is firm
and frail, too
it jumps into doubt
from certitude
           and back again
on a breeze so slight
a leaf it barely moves

I recite

Legions of saints
pass before me
they will not sit with doubt
on the breath that moves
through silence
into separation from
their heart's Desire

Photograph

I hired someone to take your picture
Meaning to place it in the paper
You were ravishing

In your ancient beauty and when
The photographer said
I needed your permission

Pondered, what could I say
To charm endearment
You've always known me

In my timidity, I turned away
From the moment.
But the photographer stood fast

Captured by the transparency
Forgetting
To ask for payment.

Contemplating dejection

Sitting in my comfortable surroundings,
encased with accumulation, I'm contemplating
dejection when I hear the voice.
  "Good morning, sir." It's a croak, nervously
he begins the story.
  "I can't hear you." He begins again.
  "I can't hear you!" His glass eye stares a line
straight through me. After I don hearing aides and
he downs a glass of water, the story proceeds.
  "Are you hungry?" He doesn't answer, just story.
  "Are you hungry?"

On the stair, he finishes his coffee.
Considering his father's bequest and funeral,
I'm not convinced of the truth of his story,
but recognise the truth of desperation: solid
as the concrete we're sitting on.
  After the tote, cap and expression of gratitude
      he lingers,
acknowledging the several years he has stopped here,
before resuming the trek south for a funeral
and the life, he hopes, will fare much better.
  I forgot to refresh his name, but I'm pretty sure
the Master sent him,
    to start me
      on the road to recovery.

Streets of Baghdád

They did not comprehend
yet gathered
    to line the streets
He would never walk again
where stones would echo centuries
    hooves of a red roan stallion.

Mothers cried aloud for their children
a mufti bewailed the state of Nasiríd-Din
and an emperor-in-waiting
    would lose a throne, refusing
to receive the Desire of Nations.
And all that
    after a declaration.

What could they possibly ask for
after paradise?

Unwanted

To their chagrin, they railed
as Unknowable revealed
as faithful kneeled.

What shall be their legacy?
What will be recalled of histories
after rejection of Him

Who fashioned them?

Paradox

i insist on nothing
but desire everything
consume undue
    moments imagining
a station near infinity
    beyond me
beyond our precious mud
dumbstruck by evidence that
    an avalanche of humanity
    in a singular body
    did collide with divinity
cloaked with the garment of affliction
chained, imprisoned, poisoned
by baser forms human

unimagined the multitude
hidden yet rising
to serve
    and adore Him

Section 4

Death &
Other Illusions

I know—no one's going to show me everything
We all come and go unknown
Each so deep and superficial
Between the forceps and the stone

—Joni Mitchell
'Hejira'

Death doth drop a short mile

It's only a door between us,
a flimsy thing of wood and air.
For me there is too much at stake
yet little, that I wouldn't dare
to keep you on the other side that door
to keep me standing here.

This is not a poem.
It's a song for the road.
It's a pack of spells to charm me
into forgetting, about not forgetting,
not to open
      the door.

I will not argue.
If you press for a commitment,
I'll just hesitate and while,
I'll talk to you in third person
      and call the song:
Death doth drop a short mile.

Death doth drop a bad boy
by ol' lady house
on his way to work, Wednesday.
He thinks I'm not paying attention,
      but I am
and don't open the door for him
      so he walked on.

Death doth sing a jack song
because he knows I love rock 'n roll
any time of day and
turn my player up really loud, to shush the road
and slap him away.
So bold am I.

Death doth sit a prim lady on the back seat,
claiming me with arched brows and
    (a)(clipped)(ac)(cent).
I listen pretty close, and
turning round to look at her, my mind walks:
how many precious children
have dropped through her sweet loins,
thinking, too: when she
    get in the car?

Death doth laugh out loud
when I stand with an ear to the door.
He knows I'm thinking, I'll keep it closed
when all he has to do is stop and give a knock
on his way to work, Wednesday,
or *any* day, he pretty please.

Death doth dream an angry snake
to slide around my ankle,
me standing with an ear to the door
    and a worry—Why's he so quiet
and slow, the other side?

Death doth send a slender Shylet,
who casts all spells, she's so beautiful.
She laughs 'cause I'm holding tight the handle
"Hell," she go, "he can just slide in the back!"
brush my shoulder with a lock of her hair
and make me forget everything,
(everything but her mouth and how she smells).
Mother of God, how'd he *do* that?
"*Gotcha!*" he laughs, front of ol' lady house.

Never mind, Shy. I'll just say goodbye
for surely, it ain't my time and anyhow,
I've a sweet wife waiting, ciao!

Death doth shine a slow smile
while I sit with my back to the door,
daring to rest and dreaming the road.
Does he suspect I'm running retreads?

Death doth glide a short mile up my hill
to catch me just as I'm about to turn the corner,
crying chocolate tears over spilt milk
and my head hurts, something fierce
because I refuse to say, give.

Death doth think a thlow thought
    as I begin the long drive home,
a thought that throws my head a meat pie,
I got only stale ham and cheese for the road,
dreaming, sweet child.

It's not fair, I say, and he knows, I *said* my prayers,
and he goes, well OK, I'll spin a story
    to get you off, this one time...
but then

Death doth chant a charmer's spell
to make me drop off to sleep
on the other side the door, thinking
    nothing at all.

He just glides through that door,
takes me in his arms, swingin' a slow sweet song,
to waltz me out the front,
dreaming his words in my ear:
    You won't feel a thing
    or cry chocolate tears—no more
    The Rose? Oh, she'll do just fine
    Anyway, she'll be along in a minute
    so you just sleep now, my beautiful boy.

Conference
ball pen

Uncle Bill

Uncle Bill was dead
before I was even aware
though he did try to take me with him
one day in leather gear,

he'd purchased for a ride
on his magnificent motorcy'
But mama said to her big brother
not with *my* son, not on your life.

Uncle Bill died on that bike
after trying to duck out of vows
with Alberta, with whom he'd slept
the previous night.

Grampa and grandma Moan
would not stand for such tripe
and the pair lived unhappily hitched
the rest of Bill's brief life.

entro p y

Is it po sible
to st p a heart
mer ly think ng it
stop d
suic de by a^{c}t of wi l
or not a$_n$ akt
j $_s$t   ntr$_o$py

He remembers a friend the day her uncle died

Moments, friend dearest,
thrown to and fro by currents
are, in truth, outrageous.
Though flavored of a bitter knife,
should not pass untasted
nay, claim them now and savor
as though the sweetest fleeing essence.
Tremble in these hours, these days!
Life and memory in fullness
while others pass in petty ways
through sieves
of dimly seen, have barely lived.

And if the whetted blade of hours
(taken in sharp relief)
will not, for guilt be broken—
'tis you who purchased with your grief
what he, with grief's bright token!

The great taxi migration

Windhoek is overrun
in a great taxi migration
Students waiting in queues for transport
to institutions of higher learning
are accompanied by bands of criminals
who escape their due with taxi accomplices

Stories of children abducted, and dropped in the veldt
stripped to their drawers, relieved of belongings
Taxis in streams from their stands into hell
indifferent to their contribution
to Armageddon

Promised

Time, if illusory, is delicate and costly
when you stretch to grasp it with old hands
as when a wood in autumn conceives
a blanket of tenderness
and all thereafter is distant promises

A rook, estranged from the flock
in leafless trees is croaking
beyond the trees and stalling
infirmities what lie in hiding there
come away, seems he is calling

Do not converse with late night voices
their every accent does betray
a sweeter one you may still find
and bring an end
to much meandering of mind

Say good night
turn down the sheets
the touch of softest cotton
reminds 'tis only the darkest winter eve
would leave you here for fallen

in the water

we collect ants in water
they parade into the kettle
        but they don't drink
they march to be cooked and perish
determined,
        they do not think
how should they?
as we (also a moment's thought)
drink ant water

While a Dark Venus

Snaring the gaze of circus males,
She is quick to remind, that male sight
Lacks specific focus (when it lights on female).

They sink like stones in the ocean,
But drown with gleeful lapping:
Eyes smear skies across a rueful smile,

That breaks with a roar, such are humid carnivores.
But thirty orbits in her wake, Venus drops one in Saturn.
Lips taste of guava or pomegranate, she offers

Her goddess mouth or invites them to the wound,
Only, they fail to impress for all their pains,
Each death more conclusive through the sequels.

Look, see! caught in her tangle,
A gallery of tragic boys who trespass
Down a primrose path, seeking deeper shadow.

Shattered
(for Pete)

Spaced
in all that acid
you jumped the bridge
& must have shattered
pretty bad

A question:
have you pulled yourself
together
or are you still falling?
I remember

San Francisco '67
you were gone already
mind blown
though I never recognized
the symptoms

didn't recognize
my own
still, I grasp at straws
attempting to imagine
how the drop felt

Beneficial tile dislocation
ball pen

Memories

Perfection will be seen with time
and the happenstance of others
as they dovetail into mine:
gestures, a smile or a glance
     give notice
        and reveal signs
that the universe has us
           on stage
jealous of position
moving in directions
we alone determine

Unison carries weight
more than the trivial:
which we write or say
is more pregnant than the vanities
that script a passion play

I'd love to name them for you
(compose another list)
but every effort would be futile
     impossible it is
to recount each slender moment
impossible, the recollection
of every stolen kiss

I pray that you, whom I have loved,
will find me in your memories and smile
     even as I,
         when I remember you

Time begs the wilderness

I.

A time in youth his back shone
with sacrifice and devotion
He walked farms in winter
and was not driven off by the slush
    of dirty snow.
He sang the frozen fields and moved
on.

Years passed, he carried
offspring to the promised land,
launching them on the high savanna:
not a drop in sight
on a sea of sand, pure as
    perfect rain
They bathed, adding laughter to
sunlight.

Decades in rank undergrowth
tangled his bootless ankles
Stumbling over memories
of audacious excursions into
    dry oshanas
He cried out
and silence answered.

In twilight he called back time
concocting verses, nocturnally
only to find his wings were soiled
and would not lift him above
    composted dreams
An angel scourged on razored plains.

II.

Desolate : sand streams
over dune crests in the Namib
all the more haunting
for the vicinity of breakers
on the Atlantic

Empty : time curls in on herself
intangible as sand carried on a sea
wind under the arcing furnace
no respite, no hopeful cumulus
only hot and cold in the same breath

Spurned : for lust matted dreams
well beyond their expiration dates
a wistful gaze at spooning pairs
undisturbed by jackals
barking while the sun sets

Unnoticed : but not alone,
a feather lights on hard sand,
blown & baked to stone
a banshee wind calls to him
and the desert sands shift

The obvious death of St. Domino

It came to pass that Domino,
patron saint of musos, lost the mastery
of his hands and fell from Rock Gibraltar
to be felled upon by wolves in cheap's clothing
and devoured within an inch of his life.

In this trial of his passion
Dom cried out, bewailing musicians' flight
who likewise fall to beasts living night
what pound synthesised beats that mince
ears and hands and other instruments
scorching a melodic world to hip hop,
the state in which you now find it.

In deafness, dayglo jesters call this art
convinced of their street credibility
when what, what it really is, is cemetery
sounding no sense or joy of melody
evoking shadows from stone.

Rise up *Oh, oh Domino*
Roll me over, Romeo, there you go
Lord, have mercy!

Tribute to illusion

Time is a multitude
Among other things, illusion
By which we keep track
Of what we owe and what is owed to us;
Incessantly checking watches & devices,
To see what time it isn't!

The notion builds mountains:
The strain whose fantasy is but fear,
That we haven't enough,
And for those too heavily invested,
Speeds the journey's end.

Therein lies the rub,
Captured by lesser and greater poets:
By the great song traveler, who went,
"He not busy being born is busy dying",
By Lord of the age, Who noted in passing,
Days allotted to us are
"Less than a fleeting moment".

We expend a lot, marking
An idea that time passes.
To the contrary!
We possess only the moment,
In which we cry and love and act
Releasing galactic power
It might serve us well to ask:
Where are we off to
In such a hurry?

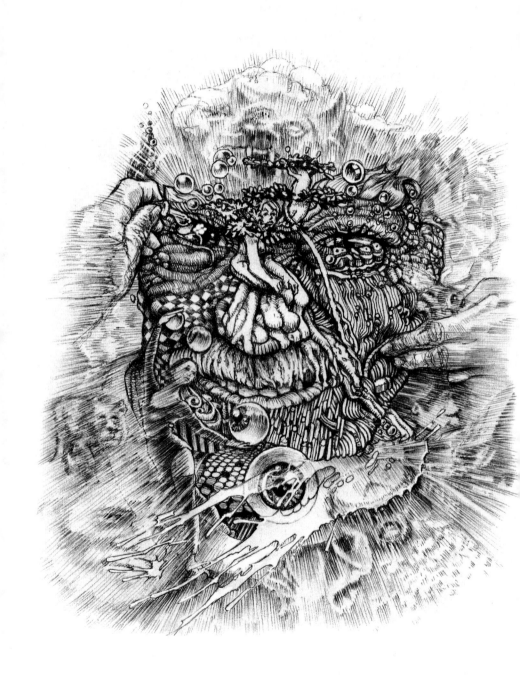

dissolution *(detail)*
ball pen and acrylic paint

Section 5
A Poet's Work

coward,clown,traitor,idiot,dreamer,beast—

such was a poet and shall be and is

—who'll solve the depths of horror to defend
a sunbeam's architecture with his life:
and carve immortal jungles of despair
to hold a mountain's heartbeat in his hand

—e. e. cummings

i believe, poets

a reflection born as prose
in its process is distilled
by an inclination to transpose
all expression into poem

I believe, poets will verify
writing is no linear occupation:
a poem is not a line simply drawn
whence it begins to eventual termination.

A poem emerges like a photograph:
to light exposed, a silver tint derives
from a dreamer's potent bath
when hung to dry, may fall apart
or call for fresh alignment,
may later yet, make another case
for a seamstress' reassignment.

So to stitching and unstitching
a search for better flow—
what should seem a moment's thought.
And though the poet may not know
how it occurred
must abide his precious war with words
for he expends life
in mortal combat with them.

Times They Are A-Changin'

It began a normal day.
The impending prom, a one and only
would be great, a double-date with Pete and Pam, and Judy.
Though his insistence, that I give a listen
didn't fit an agenda of orchid corsage and a pink Lincoln,
for the sake of friendship, I gave in, and Pete placed the first disc
reverently in my hands.
'You're No Good' comes howling and laughing, good Lord,
the man can't sing!
Does my tie hang straight? Do my shoes still shine?
I shut down the sonic assault that's crashing the party
and put the re-sheathed weapon back in Pete's hands.
He pushes back, "keep 'em for the weekend."
Prom night proceeds, without further irritation.

How deep, how important can any Sunday be?
Half conscious, I'm drifting, drifting through
homework, radio and long-plays
from '64, '63 and '62.
He sports a bulbous, gut punch of a name
        (lifted from the Welshman who killed himself with booze).
Maybe he was smitten, or had a vision of words as yet unwritten,
he's funny, comically scruffy—but seriously, is that a style,
the explosion on his head?
It's impossible to concentrate with the racket,
so I close my book and tune in the stream of lyrics instead:
untutored, nasal over pulsating guitar and a freight-train harp.
In a world of Orbison and The Beatles, none of this fits,
but some *thing* in the words holds on, and lashes me to it.
I know nothing about protest,
don't recognise 'Masters of War' or *"it's a hard rain..."*
But they spew out, undermining, compelling,
a beast of mayhem in pre-acid consciousness.
My head's doing something, and somewhere in the first or second, I go
        "Omigod, this... is incredible!"
I spun those discs into the night: two times 13 tracks, not unusual,
The Times They Are A-Changin', ten tracks over five,
over seven minutes, unavoidable,

but this is not pop—and love songs? Only ironically so.
The impossible voice drones on about God and the nation
(the military has yet to dawn on my horizon).
I'm still just a red-blooded, outwardly contented
future senior-class presidented, lover of girls.

Fifty two years hence
and as far as I can see
        things haven't changed much,
though they do, constantly:
kids tell us what they think and learn whatever;
the nation retreats, humiliated, and retreads, exchanging
magnanimity for bigotry (maybe a hard rain's still gonna...)
I see all that and puzzle how these words, these songs
(in the minds of some) contributed more to end a war
—the war, that *wasn't* one, only death to thousands on thousands
by executive action, the only way to short the constitution—
and you don't count bodies, when God's on your side—
OK, but do they make for literature, or boss poetry?
        The answer, my friend, is blowin' in the wind
and anger in the face of grab and corruption, to what end?
They don't move capital or shift its place in the sun.
So, in the absence of change, a committee honors grating lines
as though they were, and vindicates ranks of nouveau intellectuals,
rewarding the voice (retrospectively)
as if it had changed, some things
that would make the world better, or just different
like literature or poetry.
Yeah, I grumble, still stirring a pot of bogus rebellion,
'cause Zimmerman, the great chameleon, is *ours*
not the property of respected institutions,
risibly, the voice of our generation (who couldn't sing)
thinking Lenny and Joni (who take the 'don't-hold-your-breath' prize)
and Lenny said,
        "Ridiculous,"
shortly before he died,
        "you can't give Everest an award for being the mountain."
Or is it anything,
                anything at all
                        but Dylan?

seven haiku before seven

i summoned your body
golden leaves dropped from the tree
the negro girl arrived

you smiled sweetly
i remember date-nut bread
dreams and all that stuff

his publisher crashed
the internet failed
he should be going

rehearsal tomorrow
a mongoose digs in the yard
so hard to get up

he rises early
the garden needs watering
the poem is not worthy

taking pen in hand
it is so quiet outside
he laughs to himself

asleep in the chair
the electricity down
the negro girl left

Poet's work

The words are not poetic, though
this certainly is a poem. Their sound
does not echo, they are just stones.

A poet's work is, tackle the one-dimensioned ghosts
of words, exhume & wrestle their assumptions
after flung by deceased and living exponents
into graves of what they stand for.

All assumption is hubris, all vanity bullets.
A respectable poet throws stones from the deck.
He would try for land, but the strand of validation
is choked with beached animals & sea vegetation.

Glimpsing the shore, he throws himself overboard,
an offering to the serpents who coil
in her dramatic declaration:
"Poets are in mortal combat with life."

Maybe there is an echo.
But whether there is or there isn't,
they are still stones.

Writing poetry

How could I possibly be seventeen
after my sixty-fifth birthday, except
that I wished it, sitting on Santa's
   knee in the mall at Woolworth's?

Santa asked, if I'd been good
and added, "You can be anyone!"
He enrolled me in a workshop,
   poetry,
where I could write anyone I wished
to be, if I believed in them.

The facilitator wore purple tights.
They looked absolutely *terrible* on
   her, which inspired me to write
   a new her, instead of a new me
(but it weren't a poem, it was an
   essay which I titled, *Purple Tights
   Don't Become Her*).

During lunch, Hank and I talked
   about the South Dakota plains
   and Kevin Costner learning
   Lakota from Doris Leader
   Charge, a teacher at Sinte Gleska.

I asked Tokeya Inajin (First to Arise)
if Kevin's Lakota were decipherable.
"Sure," he said, "if you watch with
   subtitles."

Tokeya Inajin is also Kevin, in a
   fresh context, who told me about

White Buffalo Calf Woman, Sun
   Dance and Crazy Horse,
whose name, *Tasunke Witko*, got
twisted in translation!
The ferocious truth:
   His Horse is Spirited.

I left the workshop early.
It didn't fit my teenage personality
which would rather hit on girls in
   minis than write poetry, which
   is for wimps anyway.

On Fields of Poetry

We met on fields of poetry
one bruised and damaged heart, I knew you not to be
though I listened as you screamed silently.
Perhaps, between our worlds was sufficient synchronicity
for each to recognise, no matter how unlikely.

Our quandary in this world
is ignorance in the mathematics of love,
in the mechanics of universal attraction.
In an obstinate pose, we refuse to learn, despite ages' instruction, that
a heart will not be coerced—cannot be pushed in this or that direction.
A heart can only be wooed and won.

The first law of nature—love's algebra permeates everything—
weaving a myriad elements into fabric, some call existence,
others the grand illusion, but by all accounts, a magnificent profusion:
progressions through and throughout themes,
limitless in permutation that we might see, in just one
it is love that holds the worlds in orbit around their infinite suns.

Magnetic mathematics factor not how delicate or how gross:
a moth's wing, a Skeleton Coast.
The fabric is one, through all time and space
though patterns, beyond our numbers are embedded,
as they be
in cycles of days and expanding galaxies.

Should an equation fail to balance (as we predicted),
we imprison our children, thinking to correct or restrain them.
Yet those glowing coals will not die to ember;
they leap to flame when fanned, igniting past, present and future.
The ancestors understood fire, in hearts once kindled,
forged iron connections, was therefore holy and always shall be.

Do not speak to me of souls, young
or souls, old;
         the domain of souls lies outside of time,
id est, chronology is not a variable in these equations.
Worth derives neither from our age, nor the roles we play
in an erring night or casually passing day
but in caring for bruised and damaged hearts.

We gathered one autumn afternoon for love of poetry.

Poetry is what happens, when nothing else can

and coming together in our united states,
shared tangles of meaning as hearts spoke,
bearing witness to the gash in our troubled histories,
acknowledging: truth cannot be bound or choked.

No one has ever explained to our satisfaction
who speaks for God.
If someone had, we would not fight among ourselves to mutual
      destruction
nor seek answer to the question: if God loves our designated 'other',
how does He love us, who are marked for distinction?
"Us and them", a concept driving us toward God's extinction.

No one has ever explained to our satisfaction
who speaks for God.
And so, it has become easier simply to deny Him
(and fashionable) than to seek a Messenger worthy of the name,
though One may be closer to us than life's vein.

You could be dead a hundred years and I would still love you.

way worse

way worse than brexit
the you-es set
a dangerous precedent
on ridiculous notions
cast in shadows
bordering on criminal
genetics of race
and 'smart' genes
wealthcare to
impoverish the poor
disown the aged
enrich the rich
and close a door
on the remnants of rational
a beautiful wall,
that's two thousand miles
at a cost of two trillion
the whole enchilada
paid for by mexicans?
did that one really
want to be president
or just get elected?
to bring in the circus and
dismantle the government
fallen in parody
the rise
of D mock racy

Ill

Tumbled down a stair
and fell ill
of a trap-door illness
baffled to be triggered
and completely invisible,
its only symptom
instant magnetism.

I once believed
I could be cured
but the cure
shared no affection.
For now
    I merely carry
a trap door in my chest
and dream
    of therapy.

Back of the book

It was a calculated stroke,
    if not obvious.
Andrei wrapped the second ed.
             with the second line in respite:
It is not the business of POETRY to be anything.
     It sure ain't the two step
     but considerably rock
like Johnny, in *The Wild One*, he goes
        "Whaddaya got?"
Was it?
     Yes, it was
        foreseeable.
Language poets get shunted to the back
where they can duck out
             or defend
their position, if ready to take the flak
and close enough between the eyes
        for target practice
     because
poetry is all they say it is
            and more
quoth concrete poet Emmett Williams.
Now
     take the saltines out of the pack
& crush them
in your sleeping bag.

re genesis *(detail)*
ball pen on digital collage

NOTES

OF LIFE AND LOVE

Heart's path. Route B1, between Windhoek and Rehoboth.

a day's wet child. Line 14, after e.e. cummings: *nobody,not even the rain,has such small hands*

Havana mosaic. An informal settlement at Goreangab, on the south side of Monte Christo Avenue in Windhoek.

named for a dream. 'Roya' (Farsi), refers to dreams experienced by visionaries and prophets.

When the bagger man. A reference to the homeless and our shared vulnerability to the vicissitudes of fortune.

ANCESTORS & OTHER VISITORS

Muhapikwa was inspired by the first screening of *The Himbas Are Shooting*, directed by Solenn Bardet, written in collaboration with the Himba of Epupa and Omuhonga, at the Franco-Namibian Cultural Centre on 11 August 2012. Lyrics rendered in Otjiherero were translated by Unotjarii Mupurua.

sing for us is based on the true story of Joree Tjiharuka, survivor of the Ovaherero diaspora. It was written to her great granddaughter, Inaambura Maharero.

Warriors in the dark. Though inspired by Lakota lore, the poem does not reflect that people's creation story.

I am African woman, after V. Hasheela, 'An African Woman', in *Women and Custom in Namibia, Cultural Practice versus Gender Equality?*, 2008, ed. Oliver C. Ruppel.

Revealed (ancestral reflection #4). See Isaiah 19:3, *The Holy Bible*.

Arc magnificent was inspired by the production, *The Journey Part II,* staged by First Rain Dance at the National Theatre of Namibia (NTN) on 29 January 2014.

Sand. The town of Kolmanskop was erected after discovery of diamonds in southern Namibia. Sturdy construction has enabled the buildings to withstand the force of strong winds. The site is preserved as a museum, its structures are derelict or in ruins, some have been partially renovated.

Ndapandula. Efundula was a rite of passage for girls of the Kwanyama people in the 19th century. Participants applied a mixture of ash to their bodies to become 'Oihanangola', or 'white things'.

Unseen. Inspired by *The Mourning*, a site-specific, collaborative work performed at the Alte Feste museum in Windhoek, September 2016. Choreographed by Trixie Munyama.

Omaere is a cultured milk prepared by the Ovaherero.

FAITH

moments of Siyyid-i-Báb. Ali Siyyid Muhammad, the Báb (Gate), Herald of the Bahá'í Faith, executed by firing squad, 9 July 1850, in Tabríz, Iran.

Magus (Who awakens), a member of a priestly caste of ancient Persia, a sorcerer. *Maji*, (derived from *Magus*), the men from the East who brought gifts to the infant Jesus (Matt. 2:1).

Áqá Khán. Mírzá Áqá Khán-i-Nuri, prime minister to Nasri'd-Din Shah, 1851-1858.

Quietude, for Christopher Aiff, 10 November 1990-4 May 2014.

God be the Glory, a decal seen on the canopy of a bakkie driving the B1 south of Keetmanshoop.

Mount Sea was inspired by a dream. See *Interstellar* (2014), directed by C. Nolan.

If I should. Text in italics is from the 'Long Obligatory Prayer' by Bahá'u'lláh.

A Personal Bethlehem. World War I produced death on a scale never before

NOTES

witnessed by humanity, inspiring W.B. Yeats to proclaim the advent of the anti-Christ, which he believed was manifested in that carnage. His poem, 'The Second Coming' was written in 1919.

Prisoners. Schoolteacher, Mahvash Sabet, spent nine years in prison because of her membership on the national administrative body of the Bahá'ís of Iran. Six other members were incarcerated with her in Tehran's Evin prison after arrest in early morning raids similar to episodes in the 1980s when scores of Iranian Bahá'ís were summarily rounded up and executed. (*Bahá'í International News, 2 September 2015*)

Rumi. Jalál'ad-Dín Muhammad Rúmí, 1207-1273.

Photograph. 'ancient beauty', refers to a title of Bahá'u'lláh. 'transparency' is an abbreviation for photographic transparency, also referred to as a slide.

Streets of Baghdád. After 10 years' banishment to Iráq, Bahá'u'lláh was banished again by the Ottoman government in April 1863. He departed Baghdád amidst dramatic lamentation of the gathered populace.

A 'mufti' is an influential Islamic jurist with authority to issue 'fatwas', binding legal opinions or sentences, according to Islamic law.

Nasiri'd-Din, king of Persia, 1848-1896.

"emperor-in-waiting" refers to Sultán 'Abdu'l-Azíz, ruler of the Ottoman Empire, 1861-1876.

Paradox. "*cloaked with the garment of affliction*", quoted from the long healing prayer by Bahá'u'lláh.

DEATH AND OTHER ILLUSIONS

Uncle Bill, modeled on 'Uncle Crip' from *Elegies for Paradise Valley* by Robert Hayden. The abbreviation, motorcy' is heard on 'The Motorcycle Song', Arlo Guthrie, 1967.

Shattered (for Pete). See Wikipedia, 'Suicides at the Golden Gate Bridge'.

The obvious death of St. Domino. Italicised lyrics are from 'Domino', Van Morrison, 1970.

Tribute to illusion. "*...busy dying*", Bob Dylan, from 'It's Alright, Ma (I'm Only Bleeding)', 1965.

"*...fleeting moment*", quoted from *The Hidden Words of Bahá'u'lláh,* from the Persian, #44.

A POET'S WORK

i believe, poets references W.B. Yeats, 'Adam's Curse', *Selected Poems*, 2000, Penguin Books.

Times They Are A-Changin', was inspired by the award of a Nobel Prize in Literature to Bob Dylan, announced on 13 October 2016.

'Lenny and Joni' are references to Leonard Cohen and Joni Mitchell.

Poet's work. Erma Hayden, wife of Robert Hayden, is quoted in *From the Auroral Darkness*, 1984, John Hatcher.

Writing poetry. Sinte Gleska (Spotted Tail) University of South Dakota.

On Fields of Poetry. The epigram, *poetry is what happens when nothing else can,* has been attributed to Charles Bukowski.

way worse. See Stephen Colbert, at www/youtube.com/watch?v=TKvAKROiwk4

Back of the book. The line, "*It is not the business...*", was lifted from 'Pretext', by Stephen Rodefer, published in *Up Late, American Poetry Since 1970*, 2nd edition, 1989, Andrei Codrescu.

Emmett Williams was a member of the Darmstadt group of concrete poets between 1957 and 1959.

"saltine" is an abbreviation of saltine (or soda) cracker.

Printed in the United States
By Bookmasters